THE SCIENCE FOR GCSE

2 MATERIALS

Different materials have different properties. They behave differently under certain physical and chemical conditions. These differences help us to use and develop materials for particular purposes. This module will help you understand more about the nature of materials so that you can recognise, understand and classify them.

Relevant National Curriculum Attainment Targets: (6), (7), (8), (10)

2.1 *Using materials*

The properties of materials

We use materials to make things for a purpose. Bricks are used to build a house, wool is used to make clothing to keep you warm. Whether a material serves its purpose, depends on its properties. The properties give us information about the material. You can measure a **physical property** to obtain information about the material. A **chemical property** also tells you about *new* materials that can be made from the material.

Look at the picture below which tells you about some of the physical and chemical properties of the materials used to make a compact disc.

physical property

chemical property

The ink shouldn't 'eat' into the plastic.

The aluminium should be shiny, smooth and easy to shape.

PET SHOP BOYS

The ink shouldn't run.

The plastic should resist corrosion.

The aluminium shouldn't oxidise.

The plastic coating has to be tough and transparent.

Compact discs 'fade out after eight years' use'

COMPACT discs, sold as the faultless successor to scratch-prone LPs and finicky tapes, are beginning to self-destruct.

The problem begins with the brashly coloured inks used to print the name of the artist and the album directly on the disc's shiny surface.

"Some of the printing inks have begun to eat into the protective plastic which covers the aluminium coating of the disc."

If the aluminum gets pitted or oxidises it fails accurately to reflect the laser from the CD player and the music is distorted. Discs used to store computer data are affected in the same way.

Compact discs have taken over from video cassettes as the fastest growing consumer electronics market. Their launch five years ago was accompanied by great claims not only for their sound reproduction, but for their virtually indestructible qualities. Nearly a million compact disc players were bought in the UK last year along with 15 million discs, which retail for around £10.99.

Two large manufacturers insist that they have found no problems with their own CDs.

"But 80 per cent of the CDs we test made by others do not come up to our specifications," said one company's spokesperson. Most of these faults were insignificant, and he estimated that "less than 1 per cent" of CDs would "self-destruct" within eight years.

An American company is working with the Japanese electronics firm to produce discs made with gold or silver that will resist corrosion or oxidation. They say some aluminium discs are wearing out within three years. Their precious metal versions are expected to cost twice as much.

. . . Would you be worried about buying CDs now?

What determines the properties of materials?

Materials are made up of millions of tiny particles. The smallest of these particles that can exist on their own are called **atoms**. One of the reasons materials have different physical and chemical properties is that they are made up of different types of atoms joined together in **molecules**. The atoms are held together by forces of attraction which are another important factor in determining the properties of materials.

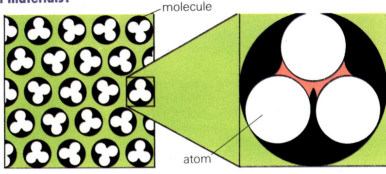

molecule

atom

Look at the picture below of the aluminium atoms in the compact disc. Can you give one example of:

a a physical property altering another physical property?

b a chemical property altering a physical property?

c a physical property helping a chemical property?

One of the factors the physical properties depend on is the weak forces of attraction between molecules.

Physical properties and chemical properties can affect each other.

One of the factors the chemical properties depend on is the strong forces of attraction inside the molecules.

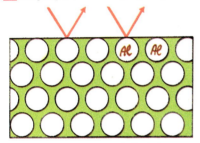

For a compact disc to do its job properly the aluminium particles must accurately reflect light from the laser.

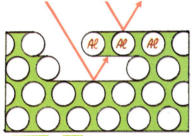

Cracks or pits in the aluminium alter its properties so the light is not reflected accurately.

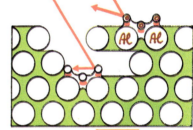

If the aluminium oxidises the physical properties are also altered. The light from the laser is not reflected. The cracks also give more opportunities for oxidation to occur.

1 Read the article on the opposite page about the compact disc.

  a What properties, highlighted in the picture of the disc, are mentioned in the article?

  b Name one advantage and one disadvantage of using gold.

  c What properties do you think the materials used to make the disc should have?

  d If the sale of compact discs stays at the level mentioned in the article, what would the faults cost the consumers over a 10 year period?

2 On the right are some comments from people involved in buying and selling CDs. Do you agree with any of the comments? What are your own thoughts about this issue?

A young retailer, who works in a record shop asked: "If I can't sell CDs with the confidence that they will last a lifetime, then I don't see the point. Vinyl will last forever."

Other browsers had a more pragmatic approach: "This won't put me off – you are bound to have wear and tear with every new product and can only discover the faults over a period of time – that has to be your expectation when upgrading to hi-tech.

"I don't think CDs were tested extensively when they were released because everybody wanted to get in on a new market, but you are buying the quality."

A student purchaser was unworried. "I don't listen to records I bought eight years ago and in eight years' time I'm not going to be listening to today's CDs, so it doesn't bother me," she said.

Shaping up

Do shapes last?

You have to apply a force in order to shape materials. This force can be such things as a pull or a stretch, a push or a squeeze. If you stretch a rubber balloon by blowing it up, it returns to its original shape when the air is let out. Materials which do this are **elastic**. Other materials such as plasticene take on new shapes. These materials are **plastic**.

Stretching ...

A material can be investigated to see if it is plastic or elastic by pulling the material out of shape. Some students did this by hanging different weights on the end of a chosen material. They used two equal lengths of the material but of different thicknesses. They found that in both cases, when the weights shown were removed, the material returned to its original shape. *It remained elastic.*

1　**a** What do the results show you about the force needed when the cross-sectional area is 2 mm², to produce the same extension as a cross sectional area of 1mm²?

　　b In each example, divide the force by the extension. What do you notice about the results in each case?

... to the limit

The students then hung more weights from the material and obtained the results given in the table below. They found that with these heavier weights the force is no longer proportional to the extension and also that the material no longer returned to its original shape when the force was removed. The material is said to be plastic. Increasing the pull even more, makes the material go more out of shape until eventually it breaks.

When a material no longer returns to its original shape, it has been permanently stretched. This permanent stretching is called **plastic deformation**. The material under investigation, of cross-sectional area 1 mm², shows plastic deformation over the range 16 N to 20 N.

Area	Force (N)	16	20	24
1 mm²	Extension (mm)	85	110	—

Why do you think the students did not measure the extension after 20 N?

*Some materials are **plastic**. They take on new shapes.*

*Some materials are **elastic**. They return to their original shape.*

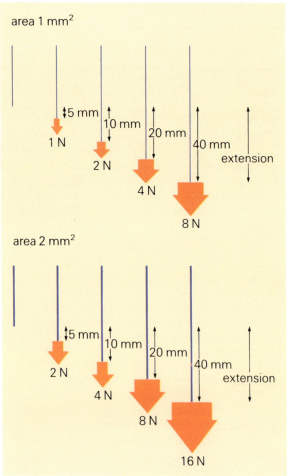

Can you see the relationship between force and extension? The force is directly proportional to the extension. As you double the force you double the extension.

Ductile and brittle

Materials which are capable of large plastic deformations are shaped more easily. Metals and some plastics can be easily shaped into useful objects for the home. Copper, for example is stretched out into long wires. Materials such as copper are said to be **ductile**. Materials which are only capable of small plastic deformations are said to be **brittle**. A brittle material usually breaks immediately when a small force is applied without first changing shape. Unlike ductile materials this means that brittle materials such as glass can be restored to their original shape by sticking the shattered bits back together again.

*Metals and some plastics are **ductile** when they are made so they can be easily shaped. Glass and pottery are also ductile when they are made but then become very **brittle** – they break easily.*

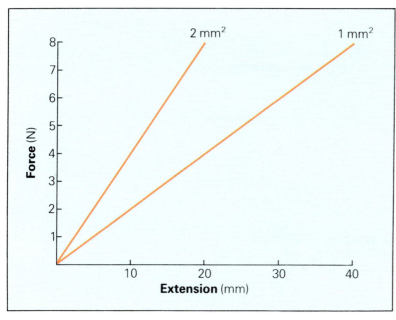

What does the graph show you about the stiffness of a material as it becomes thicker?

Resistance to stretching

Different elastic materials stretch by different amounts when a force is applied.

Stiffness is a measure of how difficult it is to change the shape of a material. The results of the stretching of the two lengths of material in the students' investigation were plotted onto this graph.

2 What is the difference between an elastic and plastic material?

3 State three things which affect the stretchiness of materials.

4 Use the results from the investigation to predict the extension for the same material when it has a cross sectional area of 2 mm^2 and heavier weights are added. Copy and complete this table.

Force (N)	16	20	24
Extension (mm)			

5 What would you expect the extension to be for a force of 8 N if the cross sectional area of the material was 4 mm^2

6 The **stress** in a material is equal to the force/ cross sectional area. What is the stress in the material under investigation on the opposite page when the force is 4 N and the area is **a** 1 mm^2 **b** 2 mm^2?

7 The **strain** in a material is equal to extension/ original length. What is the strain in the material under investigation of thickness 2 mm^2 when the force is 4 N if its original length was 1 metre?

Conductors and insulators

Energy on the move

Different materials can be used to control the movement of energy . . . . .

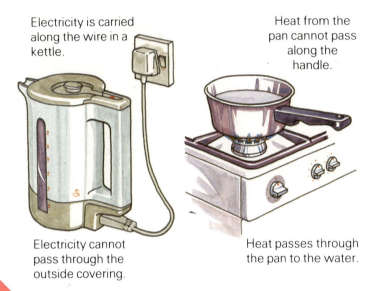

Electricity is carried along the wire in a kettle.

Heat from the pan cannot pass along the handle.

Electricity cannot pass through the outside covering.

Heat passes through the pan to the water.

Heat from the kitchen cannot pass into the fridge.

Heat and electricity are useful forms of energy but to make full use of them you have to control their movement.

Conductors and insulators

Materials which allow energy to pass along them are called **conductors**, those which do not are called **insulators**. The ability of a material to allow energy to pass along it is measured by its **conductivity**. The higher the conductivity of a material the more easily energy passes along the material. The ability of a material to allow *electrical* energy to pass along it is measured by its **electrical conductivity**. The ability of a material to allow *heat* energy to pass along it is measured by its **thermal conductivity**. Metals such as copper and silver are good conductors of heat and electricity. Materials such as glass and air are **insulators**. They do not allow energy to pass along as easily as conductors.

Material	Thermal conductivity $(Wm^{-1}k^{-1})$
silver	420
copper	385
stainless steel	150
glass	1.2
water	0.6
wood	0.2
air	0.03

What does the table show you about thermal conductivity of metals compared to other materials?

The heat transfer in gases, ...

The transfer of heat energy in materials takes place when particles with lots of energy collide with particles which have less. On collision, energy is transferred. The greater the number of collisions, the more efficient is the transfer of energy. The number of collisions is increased if the particles are close together or moving very fast. The diagram shows you how energy is transferred in gases. What does it show you about how often gas particles collide?

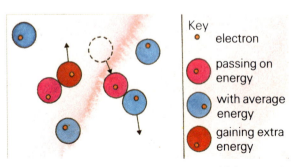

Key
- electron
- passing on energy
- with average energy
- gaining extra energy

In gases the particles move fast but are widely spaced apart. They are not very good at transferring heat energy.

...solids and liquids

Solids and liquids are much better at transferring energy than gases. What do these diagrams show you about the number of collisions in liquids and gases compared with solids?

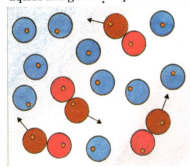

Liquids have particles which are much closer together than gases. They move around much less than those in gases. Although there are some collisions there are not enough to make them good conductors of heat.

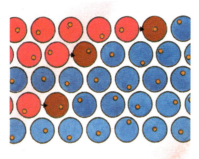

Non metal solids have particles which are much closer than gases. They don't move but transfer energy by vibrating about a fixed position. They are not as good as liquids at transferring heat.

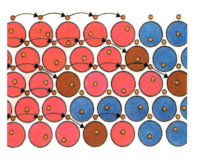

The particles of all materials contain electrons. In a metal, although these electrons are quite far apart, some are free to move. Heat energy causes these 'free' electrons to move about and collide with the larger particles making them vibrate – so they are very good at transferring heat energy.

Electrical transfer

Electrical energy is transferred by electrons passing electrical energy along a wire in an electrical circuit. The arrangement of electrons in metals means that they contain many more free electrons than most other materials. This makes them very good conductors of electricity. Some of the fast-moving free electrons eventually collide with the larger particles in the metal and lose their energy as heat.

Like any other material, the ability of a metal to allow electrons to pass electrical energy is measured by its **electrical conductivity**. At very low temperatures some materials have extremely low electrical conductivity. **Superconductors** are materials such as these in which the number of electrons colliding with other particles has been very much reduced. **Semi conductors**, like silicon, contain *less* free moving electrons than conductors but more than insulators.

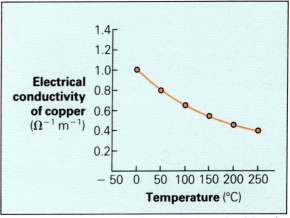

The graph shows you that the electrical conductivity of a metal decreases with increase in temperature. What does it tell you about the number of collisions the electrons make with the other particles as the temperature increases?

1 **a** Why do stainless steel pans have copper bottoms?
  b Why do some cooking pans have wooden handles?
  c Animals have fur or feathers to keep them warm. Explain how they keep the animals warm.
  d How many times better an insulator is air than glass?

2 Look at the diagrams and use them to explain
  a why water is a better conductor of heat than wood.
  b why non-metal solids are bad conductors of electricity.

3 Look at the graph above.
  a What is the electrical conductivity of copper at 75°C?
  b What do you think the electrical conductivity will be at 50°C?

4 Explain why metals are better conductors of electricity at low temperatures than at high temperatures.

Strength and hardness

Strong stuff

A strong material is one which is difficult to break when you apply a **force**. This force could be a pull such as a climber would use to test a climbing rope. Or it could be a squeeze like you give to an empty coke tin, or a crushing blow like a builder might use to break up stone slabs when making crazy paving.

A material which is difficult to break by pulling is said to have good **tensile strength**. One which is difficult to break by crushing is said to have good **compressive strength**. When materials are being bent, they are squashed and squeezed at the same time. To resist bending materials need good tensile *and* good compressive strength.

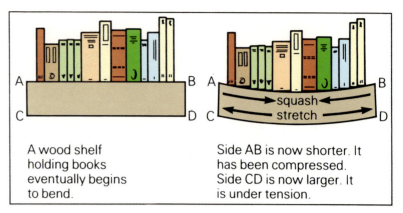

A wood shelf holding books eventually begins to bend.

Side AB is now shorter. It has been compressed. Side CD is now larger. It is under tension.

What does strength depend on?

A group of students decided to investigate how the length and thickness of wool alters its strength. The threads they used and the maximum forces they found they could bear before breaking are shown here.

> Why do you think the students were able to conclude that the length of the wool didn't matter?

Although the force varied for the threads, the force per unit area (e.g. 2 N/1 mm^2; 2 N/1 mm^2; 8 N/4 mm^2) or the **stress** was the same. The stress that a material can stand, provides a measure of its strength and not the force applied.

Look at the diagram showing the results of a compression test on a piece of concrete. What forces are needed to break the test pieces B and C?

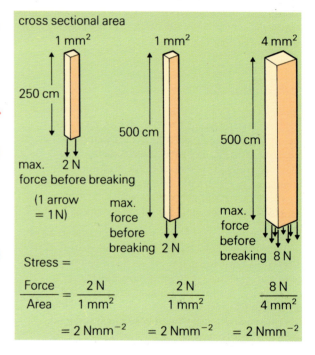

cross sectional area

1 mm^2 1 mm^2 4 mm^2

250 cm   500 cm   500 cm

max. 2 N
force before breaking

(1 arrow = 1N)

max. force before breaking 2 N

max. force before breaking 8 N

Stress =

$$\frac{\text{Force}}{\text{Area}} = \frac{2\,N}{1\,mm^2} \qquad \frac{2\,N}{1\,mm^2} \qquad \frac{8\,N}{4\,mm^2}$$

$$= 2\,Nmm^{-2} \quad = 2\,Nmm^{-2} \quad = 2\,Nmm^{-2}$$

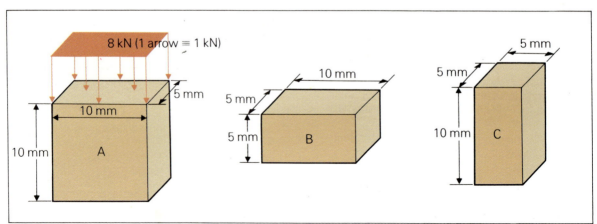

8 kN (1 arrow ≡ 1 kN)

5 mm

10 mm

10 mm   A

5 mm   10 mm   5 mm   B

5 mm   5 mm   10 mm   C

A force of 8 kN, applied over the whole area, was required to break test piece A.

What happens on stretching?

Solid materials are made of particles packed very closely together. These particles are held together by forces of attraction.

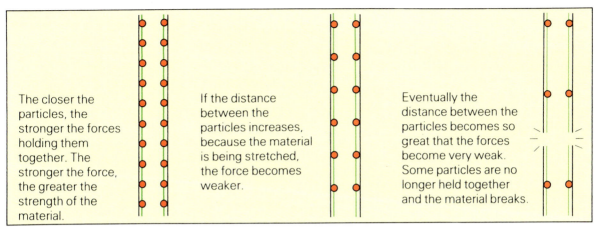

The closer the particles, the stronger the forces holding them together. The stronger the force, the greater the strength of the material.

If the distance between the particles increases, because the material is being stretched, the force becomes weaker.

Eventually the distance between the particles becomes so great that the forces become very weak. Some particles are no longer held together and the material breaks.

The forces of attraction between particles in a solid are weakened, eventually to breaking point, if the material is stretched.

Hardness

If the forces of attraction between the particles in a solid are very powerful, the material is said to be **hard**. A typical property of a hard material is that it is difficult to scratch. A harder material will always scratch a softer material so that the harder material can be made into a good cutting tool and will cut through the softer material.

Study the following information about the relative hardness of five materials then answer question 5.

Tungsten carbide will drill through **wood** and **steel**.

Diamond will drill through **tungsten carbide** and **steel**.

Wood can be scratched or marked by **glass**.

Both **steel** and **tungsten carbide** will scratch **glass**.

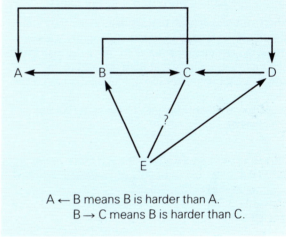

A ← B means B is harder than A.
B → C means B is harder than C.

The five materials, tungsten carbide, wood, steel, diamond and glass are represented in this diagram by labels A, B, C, D, E.

---

1. What is the difference between strength and hardness?

2. Look at the diagram showing the testing of the tensile strength of wool.
   a What force would be needed to break wool if its cross-sectional area was 2 mm²?
   b Why would the length of wool change during the experiment? Would this effect the results?

3. A weight of 60 N has to be hung from a piece of polythene of cross-sectional area 4 mm² in order to break it. What is the tensile strength of the polythene?

4. a Why does a material stretch when it is under tension?
   b Why does increasing the thickness of a material increase its tensile strength?

5. a Is material C harder or softer than material E?
   b Identify the labels A, B, C, D, E belonging to the five materials.
   c Arrange the materials in order of increasing hardness, starting with the hardest first.

Toughening up

Energy storers and releasers

Many materials can store energy when their shape is stretched or squeezed but only elastic materials can release this energy and return to their original shape.

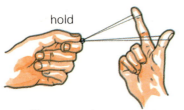

If you pull a piece of string it will stretch a bit. But a rubber band will stretch a long way. Energy has been used to stretch the rubber band.

. . The energy is stored in the rubber band . .

. . . When you let go of the rubber band energy stored in the band can be used to propel an object. The rubber band returns to its original shape.

Tough and brittle materials–energy users

When a force is applied to some materials, they will absorb a lot of energy by deforming slightly without breaking. The energy is 'used' to cause the material to go out of shape. These materials are said to be **tough**. Other materials such as ceramic break easily when a force is applied to them. The energy is 'used' to make cracks grow bigger. These materials are said to be **brittle**

The table shows a variety of tough and brittle materials. Are all the metals in the table tough materials?

Material	Tensile strength (MNm^{-2})	% Stretch before breaking
copper	215	60
concrete	5	0
cast iron	200	0
steel	700	20
ceramic	150	0
lead	20	60

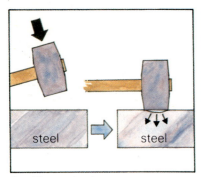

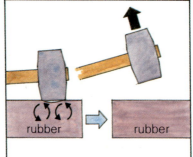

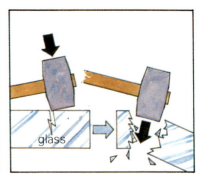

Steel is tough – it can absorb energy. The absorption of the energy causes the shape of the material to be permanently changed. Copper and brass are also tough materials that behave like steel.

Thick rubber is tough – it absorbs energy because it is elastic. The absorbed energy is released back to the hammer and the shape of the rubber is restored. Thick polythene sheeting and nylon are also tough materials that behave like rubber.

Glass is brittle – it is a poor absorber of energy. It can only resist a force provided there is no weakness in its structure. Energy from the hammer causes a crack, usually in the shortest direction through the material. If enough energy is supplied, it acts along the crack causing the glass to break. Ceramic tiles, cast iron and bricks are also brittle materials.

Toughening up

Brittle materials can be made tougher if you can stop them cracking. In order to do this brittle materials are combined with a material made of fibre. Energy usually acts on brittle materials by causing a crack across the shortest distance but with the addition of the fibre the energy is transferred through the material in a different direction – along the fibres. A natural example of this is wood which consists of cellulose fibres, which can be seen as grains in the wood, held together by **lignin** (see 2.13).

Using the same principle brittle materials such as plaster and some plastics can be made tougher by the synthetic addition of fibres. Its even possible to combine two brittle materials – as long as one is in the form of a fibre – and end up with a tough material! Glass reinforced plastic (GRP) contains glass fibre in a brittle plastic resin – this is an extremely useful synthetic composite, used for boats, storage tanks, pipes, low temperature engine parts because it is light and tough.

Wood is a tough material. It takes a lot of energy to chop through a tree trunk.

The bottom section of the bridge is being stretched by the weight of the cars passing over it. Concrete is brittle when it is stretched and can crack.

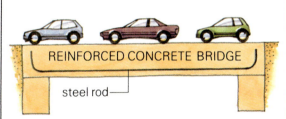

The steel rods act like fibres. Energy being used to try and crack the concrete is passed along the steel rods instead.

The principle of combining a brittle material with another material to prevent cracking is used in reinforced concrete.

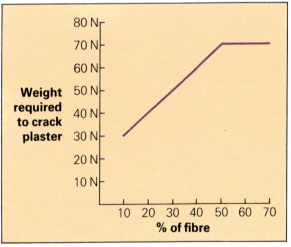

The graph shows the results of toughness tests on plaster. Why do you think the graph does not pass through the origin?

1 Give one useful example of an elastic material as an energy storer and releaser.

2 Why is it safer to have the front of cars made of tough materials?

3 **a** Which of the materials given in the table are tough and which are brittle?
   b Arrange the tough materials in order of toughness, starting with the toughest first.
   c Which of the following statements are true of the materials in the table? Tough materials are very strong. Brittle materials are very weak.

4 Do all tough materials go out of shape when they are subjected to a force?

5 Look at the graph of the toughness of plaster.
   a State three conditions needed to make the test fair.
   b What weight is needed to break the plaster when it contains **a** 20% fibre? **b** 10% fibre?
   c Sketch a graph showing what you think the result would look like if the thickness of the fibre was doubled in the plaster, given the same range of weights.

Mass and weight

*A box of golf balls has more matter in it than a box of table tennis balls. It has greater **mass**.*

A massive problem

You are made of millions of tiny particles called **atoms**. In fact everything is made up of these atoms. Some atoms contain more "stuff" or matter in them than others. We say that the atoms have different **masses**. The more matter they have in them, the greater the mass. Your mass is the sum of all the masses of each of the atoms of which you are made. The mass of an object is measured in kilograms (kg) . . . but how can you measure the masses of millions of atoms to find your total mass?

An attractive feeling

There is a natural effect which you feel all the time although you may not think about it, that can be used to measure mass. This effect is the pull between the mass of any object on Earth (e. g. you!) and the mass of the Earth. We call this pull **the force due to gravity**. This force is the same for both the Earth and you (the object).

If two objects are close together, there is always a force of attraction between them. The size of the force depends on the mass of both objects. The greater the mass, the greater the force of attraction between them. For most objects, their mass is so small that this force is not noticeable. However there are other objects in our solar system – planets, moons, which also have very large masses. These masses are so large that, like Earth, their force of attraction is felt – they have their own force due to gravity.

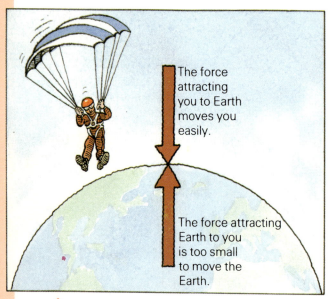

The force attracting you to Earth moves you easily.

The force attracting Earth to you is too small to move the Earth.

▲ *What does this drawing show you about how a planet's pull on an object depends on its mass?*

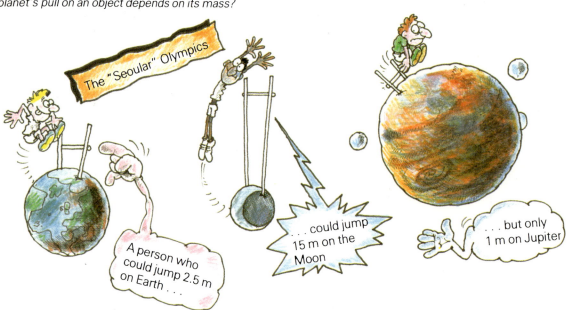

Balancing the problem

The force due to gravity can be used to measure the **mass** of an object on Earth because the greater the mass of the object the greater the force due to gravity.

The Earth pulls a mass of 1 kilogram to it with a force of 9.8 newtons (N). The force due to gravity can be used to measure the mass of an object. You can measure the Earth's pull on an object easily, using for example a top pan balance. The Earth's pull on an object is called its **weight**. The Earth's pull on an object of mass 1 kg is 9.8 newtons, i.e. it *weighs* 9.8 N. If your mass is 30 kg, you weigh nearly 300 N (30 × 9.8).

Remember that mass and weight are *two different things* although we use weight to measure mass.

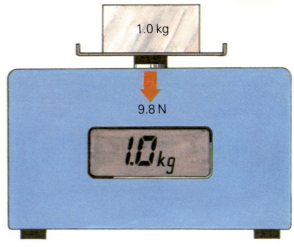

The balance moves because the mass exerts a force in newtons (N) and this force is used to indicate the mass directly in kilograms (kg).

Constant mass but changing weight

An object contains the same type and number of atoms no matter where it is in our solar system. This means the mass of an object is the same on any planet in our solar system.

The weight of an object depends on the pull or force of gravity on it. The planets have different masses so they have different pulls on an object. This means the weight of an object will vary, depending on which planet it is on. Unlike mass, weight is not constant through our solar system.

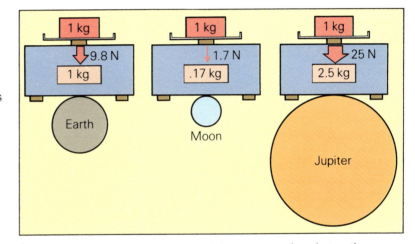

The force of gravity on Earth is about 6 times greater than that on the moon and about 2.5 times less than that on Jupiter.

1 Why does 1 litre of neon have a mass 5 times that of helium when they both have the same number of atoms?

2 How high do you think the person in the figure, who can jump 2.5 m on Earth, would be able to jump on Mars where the force due to gravity is 0.4 times that on Earth?

3 What is the mass of an object if its weight on Earth is 196 N?

4 Look at the data and then answer the following questions **a** – **c**.

Planet	Force acting on mass of 1 kg
Earth	9.8 N
Moon	0.17 N
Jupiter	2.5 N
Mars	0.4 N
Neptune	1.25 N

a An object of mass 5 kg has a weight 2 N on which planet?

b What would be the mass and the weight of this same object on Earth?

c If you lived on Jupiter, where could you go if you wanted to lose half your weight? Would you have to buy a new set of clothes?

5 Look at this data on the Earth's gravitational pull that could have been taken from a spacecraft.

Distance from centre of Earth	R	$2R$	$3R$
Force	9.8	2.45	1.1

a What 2 factors does gravitational pull depend on?

b What would be the gravitational pull at a distance $4R$ from the Earth?

c Would the spacecraft ever be completely weightless?

2.6

Heavyweights and lightweights

Heavy stuff!

You can tell if an object is heavy because it is difficult to lift or carry. However, heaviness is a property of the *object* and not necessarily of the material of which it is made. You can compare the heaviness of two objects by putting them at each end of a see-saw.

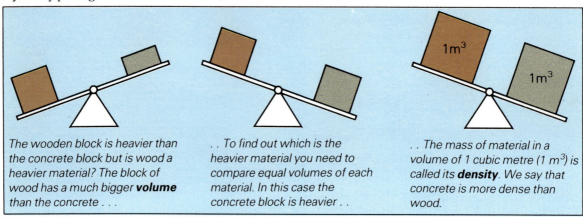

*The wooden block is heavier than the concrete block but is wood a heavier material? The block of wood has a much bigger **volume** than the concrete . . .*

. . To find out which is the heavier material you need to compare equal volumes of each material. In this case the concrete block is heavier . .

*. . The mass of material in a volume of 1 cubic metre (1 m³) is called its **density**. We say that concrete is more dense than wood.*

A dense situation

All materials are made up of tiny particles called atoms. The **density** of a material depends on the number of particles in one cubic metre and the mass of each particle. How does the picture help to explain why lead is the most dense material and sulphur the least?

Metals such as lead contain heavy particles which are packed closely together.

. . . Other metals like aluminium also contain tightly packed particles but they are not as heavy . . .

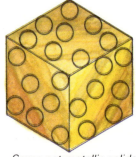

. . Some not-metallic solids for example sulphur, contain particles of about the same mass as aluminium. They are, however, not as tightly packed.

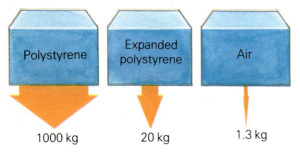

The density of materials can be altered by changing the number of particles.

Changing density

Materials can be made less dense by having fewer particles in a cubic metre or by replacing some of the particles by lighter ones. Polystyrene is a plastic material used widely in packaging as expanded polystyrene. Expanded polystyrene is made by blowing air into molten polystyrene. Look at the data which shows the masses of 1 cubic metre of three materials. What does it show you about the number of particles in *expanded* polystyrene compared with polystyrene?

Sinkers . .

Whether an object sinks or floats in a liquid depends on the density of the material of the object compared to the density of the liquid. Look at the pictures which shows you why an object sinks. What type of liquid would have to replace the water in order to stop the object sinking?

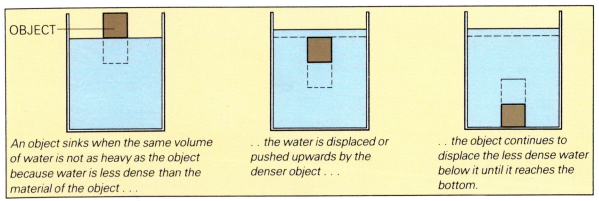

An object sinks when the same volume of water is not as heavy as the object because water is less dense than the material of the object . . .

. . the water is displaced or pushed upwards by the denser object . . .

. . the object continues to displace the less dense water below it until it reaches the bottom.

. . . risers and floaters

Rising is the reverse process to sinking. Look at the pictures which show you why an object rises then floats. Helium is less dense than air. What change would you notice if the bubble had been filled with helium instead of air?

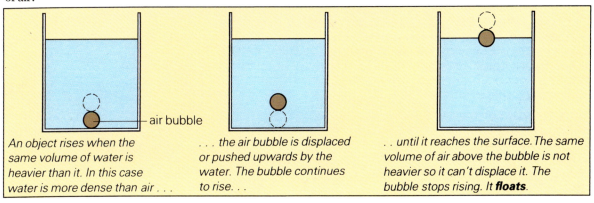

An object rises when the same volume of water is heavier than it. In this case water is more dense than air . . .

. . . the air bubble is displaced or pushed upwards by the water. The bubble continues to rise. . .

. . until it reaches the surface. The same volume of air above the bubble is not heavier so it can't displace it. The bubble stops rising. It **floats**.

1. The density of wood is four times less than that of concrete. What volume of wood is needed to balance a 0.5 m³ concrete block on the see-saw?

2. Why is copper a denser material than iron when the number of particles of each in 1 m³ is about the same?

3. Material A has particles 5 times heavier than material B. Material B has 10 times more particles. If the density of material A is 10 kg/ m³, what is the density of material B?

4. A block of lead, mass 100 g, was lowered into a measuring cylinder containing 50 cm³ of water. If the final level of water was 59 cm³, what is the density of lead in g/cm³? The same piece of lead was lowered into a measuring cylinder containing mercury. The level only rose 8 cm³. What has happened and what is the density of the mercury?

5. Look at the data on the densities of some gases given in kg/m³.

Helium	0.175
Neon	0.9
Air	1.29
Argon	1.8
Carbon dioxide	1.9

a If balloons were filled with each gas which ones would rise in air?

b A balloon sinks in neon but floats in argon. What gas could it contain?

c Breathed out air contains more carbon dioxide than breathed in air. When you blow up a balloon, why doesn't it float in the air?

d In a volume of 1 m³ there are the same number of gas particles. How many times heavier are argon atoms than neon atoms?

Expansion and contraction

Getting bigger

Some materials increase in size or **expand** when they are heated. They decrease in size or **contract** when they are cooled.

Materials are made up of particles which are moving or vibrating.

When a material is heated it gains energy which causes the particles to move or vibrate even more.

What do these pictures show you about the increase in size or expansion of solids, liquids and gases compared to each other?

Although you can't see the expansion, a metal lid can expand. It sometimes gets stuck in a kettle when it contains very hot water.

Solids – same shape, different size

The expansion of materials takes place in all directions. Solid materials have a fixed volume and shape. When a solid block expands, the fractional increase in length is the same for the width and breadth. There is an increase in size *but no change in shape*.

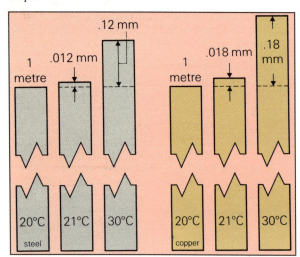

The increase in size of a solid bar is more noticeable along the longest part – its length. The amount of expansion depends on the type of material, the length of the bar and how hot it becomes.

Gases expand greatly on heating to fill any space available to them.

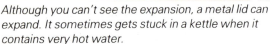

The expansion of a liquid inside a thermometer can be seen when the temperature rises.

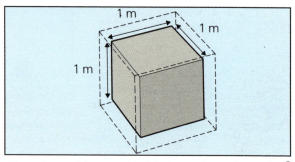

The volume of this steel block is 1 m × 1 m × 1 m = 1 m^3. If it is heated by 10°C its new volume is 1.000 12 m × 1.000 12 m × 1.000 12 m = 1.000 36 m^3.

*Strips of metal can be made by joining together two different metal materials. This is called a **bimetallic strip** . . .*

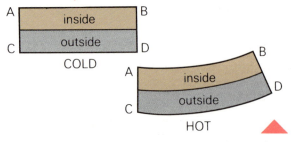

. . If the bimetallic strip is heated one metal expands more than the other. Both AB and CD have expanded but CD has expanded more than AB so the strip bends. If the bimetallic strip were made of steel and copper which do you think would be on the outside?

Liquids – different shapes and sizes

Liquids have a fixed volume but no fixed shape. They take up the shape of their container. When a liquid is heated its expansion is channelled by the shape of the container. This expansion could make a liquid change its shape. To calculate the total amount of expansion of a liquid you have to know the increase in volume of 1 cm³ of the liquid for every °C rise in temperature. Equal volumes of different liquids will expand by different amounts for the same rise in temperature. What does this picture show you about the amount of movement of particles in alcohol compared with water and mercury?

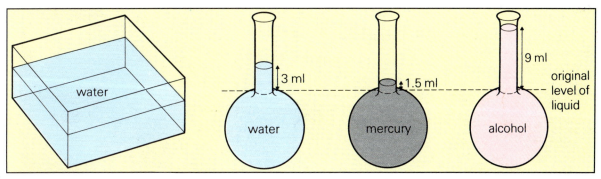

Heating the same volume of water in a different shaped container can mean that the expansion that has occurred is easier to see.

To compare the expansion of different liquids containers of the same shape and volume are used. Each flask shown here contained 1 litre of liquid heated by 10°C.

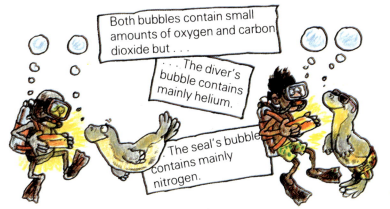

Both bubbles contain small amounts of oxygen and carbon dioxide but . . .

. . . The diver's bubble contains mainly helium.

. . . The seal's bubble contains mainly nitrogen.

If both bubbles were about the same size in the cold waters of the Arctic . . . .

Gases – all shapes and sizes

Gases have no fixed shape or volume but they can be trapped in something like a balloon or a gas bubble. Look at the pictures. What do they show you about the amount of expansion of different gases?

◀ *. . they would still be about the same size as each other in the warm waters of the Caribbean but each about 10% bigger.*

---

1 Glass expands by 0.008 mm for every °C rise in temperature. How much would a sheet of glass, 1 m by 2 m, expand by if it were heated by 10°C?

Why could this be a problem in winter?

2 What would be the new volume of the 1 m³ steel block shown in the figure if it were heated by **a** 20°C **b** 100°C?

3 British Rail fits metal tyres of 0.8 m diameter onto wheels 1 m diameter.
  a Suggest ways they could do this.
  b What will happen to the tyres when they heat up during braking?
  c How can you make sure the tyres won't fall off during braking?.

4 **a** Why do you think the capillary tubes for alcohol thermometers are thicker than those for mercury?
  b Mercury is much heavier than water and alcohol. Do you think it is a fair test to compare the expansion of equal volumes but different masses of liquids?
  c What is the maximum volume of water at 20°C you could pour into 1000 cm³ beaker and heat to 70°C without it overflowing?

5 A 1 metre length of gold expands by 0.014 mm for every °C rise in temperature. By how much would a gold bar 0.1 m by 0.01 m by 0.01 m expand in the waters of the Caribbean if they were 30°C warmer than the Arctic?

Changing state

What a state!

These three photographs show changes in the properties of a common substance. What changes in the properties can you see that have taken place? Why do you think the substance has changed in this way?

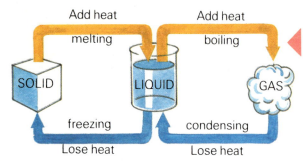

Different states

The boiling kettle and the frozen pondwater above show how the same substance, water, can be changed by heating and cooling. Steam and ice are clearly different from the liquid you see when you turn on a tap. By changing the temperature of water it can become a solid (ice) or a gas (steam).

Solids, liquids and gases are called the **three states of matter**. Ice, water and steam are all different states of the same substance – water. The change from one state to another can be reversed: water freezes to ice and ice can melt back to water.

Getting things moving

The particles which make up a solid are very close to each other and do not move away from their fixed position as they are held by other particles around them. When a solid is heated, its particles gain energy, causing them to break free from their fixed position and begin to move around. This causes solids to melt into liquids. The temperature at which this happens is called the **melting point**.

By making the particles of a substance move about more rapidly, solids become liquids and liquids become gases. When water is heated its particles gain enough energy to escape from the liquid into the air. This happens slowly when water is heated by the sun and **evaporates** from the pavement after a shower of rain. It can happen quickly when water is heated until it boils. When a substance boils, bubbles of gas form inside the liquid and rise to the surface. The temperature at which this happens is called the **boiling point**. Evaporation can happen below the boiling point.

In a solid the particles are very close and they do not move away from their fixed position.

In a liquid the particles are further apart. They have more energy and move.

In a gas particles are very far apart. They move around rapidly in all directions.

Stopping things moving

When a gas is cooled, the movement of particles slows down. Eventually this causes the gas to stop moving around so much and stay in a fairly fixed position. When this happens the gas **condenses** into a liquid. Similarly, when a liquid is cooled sufficiently to *stop* its particles moving it freezes and becomes solid. By lowering the temperature to slow down the movement of molecules, gases become liquids and liquids become solids.

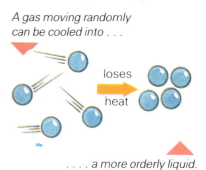

A gas moving randomly can be cooled into . . .

loses heat

. . . . a more orderly liquid.

Making use of different boiling points

The difference in the boiling points of substances can be used to separate liquids from one another. The flask in the diagram contains a mixture of two liquids. It takes only a little energy to make the smaller molecules move around enough to become gases. When the mixture is heated the liquid made from smaller molecules boils first. The water cools the vapour and so vaporisation is followed by condensation back to a liquid which only contains the small molecules. So the two parts or fractions of the mixture have been separated because of their different boiling points. This process is called **fractional distillation**.

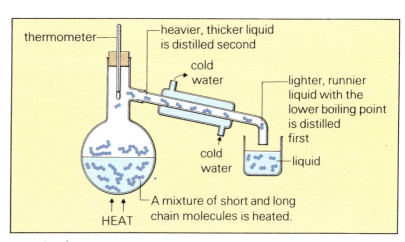

*Liquid hydrocarbon mixtures with different boiling points can be separated by **fractional distillation**.*

Looking at properties

The table opposite shows the properties of a group of chemicals called **hydrocarbons**. These molecules are made from hydrogen and carbon atoms joined together in a chain. The length of the molecule depends on the number of carbon atoms that make up the chain. The length of the molecule affects the runniness, **viscosity**, of a liquid eg. petrol is more viscous than paraffin. A liquid can be made less viscous by heating.

Even though these different hydrocarbons are each made up of molecules of hydrogen and carbon atoms their properties differ because the lengths of their molecules differ.

Name of hydrocarbon	Number of carbon atoms in the	Boiling point °C	State at room temperature (21°C)
ethane	2	− 88	gas
butane	4	0	?
petrol	5 to 10	20 to 70	runny liquid
Paraffin	10 to 16	120 to 240	thick liquid
Lubricating oil	20 to 70	250 to 350	?

1. Why does steam turn back to water when it hits a cold window?

2. At room temperature in what state will the following substances be:
   a butane **b** lubricating oil?

3. Propane is a hydrocarbon containing 3 carbon atoms in its molecules. From the information given in the table above give an estimate of its boiling point.

4. **a** What happens to the boiling point of hydrocarbons when the length of their molecules increases?
   b Explain why the size of molecules affects the boiling point of a substance.

2.9

From the sea to your home

Crude oil naturally occurs beneath the sea or ground. It is an important source of many chemicals so it is much sought after. Once it is discovered it is extracted on a large scale by drilling.

Black, smelly and valuable

Crude oil is a sticky, black, smelly liquid that lies beneath the Earth's crust, particularly in areas such as the North Sea and the Gulf region of the Middle East. It is not very useful in its raw state but it is the source of many of the chemicals that we use everyday.

Nearly all the substances that are found in crude oil are **hydrocarbons**. These different hydrocarbons need to be separated out so that they can be used for different purposes. Look at the diagrams below and refer back to 2.9. How can the difference in boiling points of the various hydrocarbons be used to separate crude oil into its different parts (**fractions**)?

1000 litres of crude oil

- 2 l of liquid propane gas
- 300 l of petrol
- 70 l of naphtha
- 100 l of paraffin
- 300 l of diesel
- 20 l of lubricating oil
- 200 l of fuel oil
- 8 l of bitumen

*Crude oil is a mixture of compounds called **hydrocarbons**.*

Mixture	No. of carbon atoms	Boiling point (°C)
L.P.G. (Liquified petroleum gas)	1 – 4	−160 to 20
Petrol	5 – 8	20 to 70
Naphtha	8 – 11	70 to 120
Paraffin (kerosine)	11 – 15	150 to 250
Diesel	15 – 19	between 250 and 350
Lubricating oil	20 – 30	
Fuel oil	30 – 40	
Bitumen	more than 40	above 350

Crude oil is a mixture of hydrocarbons with different molecular chain lengths. As the chain length increases so does the boiling point.

Separating the mixture

At oil refineries crude oil is separated into its different parts by a process called fractional distillation. You may have used this process to separate liquids in the laboratory but as you can imagine the industrial process is on a much larger scale. The process is carried out in oil refineries in huge fractionating towers.

In a fractionating tower crude oil is heated by a furnace and the gases that are produced pass into the tower. The temperature is highest (about 350°C) at the bottom of the tower and lowest (about 70°C) at the top. The various gases rise up the tower, the smaller the molecule, the *lower* the temperature at which it boils. Those with smaller molecules, such as naphtha, will condense back to liquid near the top of the tower at about 70°C. Those with larger molecules, such as fuel oil, will condense back to liquids soon after the temperature goes below 350°C near the bottom of the tower. LPG will still be a gas at the top of the tower since it condenses at a temperature much lower than 70°C.

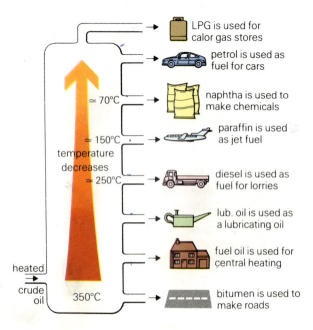

LPG is used for calor gas stores

petrol is used as fuel for cars

naphtha is used to make chemicals

paraffin is used as jet fuel

diesel is used as fuel for lorries

lub. oil is used as a lubricating oil

fuel oil is used for central heating

bitumen is used to make roads

≈ 70°C

≈ 150°C

temperature decreases

≈ 250°C

350°C

heated crude oil

Using the different fractions

In general, fractions made of larger molecules have higher boiling points and also tend to be heavier, less runny and harder to evaporate than fractions containing smaller molecules. What does the table show you about how the properties of each fraction link with its use?

The fractions have different properties. The different properties give rise to different uses. ▼

Fraction	Properties at room temperature	Use
Liquified petroleum gas	It is a colourless gas and is highly flammable.	Used as a fuel for calor gas stoves
Petrol	It is a free flowing liquid that is easily vapourised. It is highly flammable.	Used as a fuel in cars.
Lubricating oil	It is a very thick liquid that will only become a vapour at very high temperatures. It is not very flammable.	Used to lubricate machinery, moving parts etc.
Bitumen	It is a solid and will melt into a sticky liquid when heated. It is not very flammable. It does not mix with water.	Used to surface roads.

Small scale distillation

The apparatus shown in the diagram can be used to distill crude oil in the laboratory. A group of students carried out this investigation and found they were able to separate three different fractions from the crude oil. Their results are shown in this table. What do you think each of the three fractions contain?

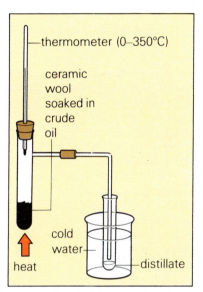

The small scale laboratory fractional distillation of crude oil.

	1st fraction	2nd fraction	3rd fraction
Boiling point (°C)	20 – 80	90 – 150	150 – 240
Appearance of fraction	pale yellow runny liquid	dark yellow fairly thick liquid	brown and very thick liquid
How the fraction burns	burns easily with clear yellow flame	harder to burn with a smoky flame	hard to burn with a very smoky flame

1. The table below shows the number of litres of some fractions of crude Arabian oil in 1000 litres.

PETROL	200 litres
DIESEL	300 litres
FUEL OIL	450 litres

   a How do you expect the smell and runniness of Arabian oil to compare with the oil in the oil drum figure. Explain your answer.

   b What is the percentage of petrol in each barrel?

2. A fraction from the distillation of crude oil has a boiling point of 160°C. What properties would you expect it to have and what would it be used for?

3. a State one use of bitumen and explain why its properties make it an ideal material for this use.

   b Give two reasons why petrol is used as a fuel in cars rather than lubricating oil.

4. Look at the results of the simple laboratory distillation.

   a What hydrocarbon mixture is present in the first fraction? Give two observations that support your prediction.

   b Smoke contains unburnt carbon. Why does fraction 1 burn clearly and fraction 3 burn with a smokey flame?

   c Predict two properties of a fourth fraction.

2.11 *From oil to plastics*

Too much or too little

The distillation of crude oil provides us with many useful products but we use these products in differing quantities. Some fractions are in great demand but are in short supply. Heavier fractions, such as fuel oil and bitumen, make up the larger proportion of some crude oils but they are not needed as much as lighter fractions such as petrol.

Fraction	Amount present in crude oil (%)	Current every day demand (%)
Liquified petroleum gas	2	4
Petrol	16	24
Naphtha	10	4
Paraffin	15	7
Diesel oil	19	23
Lubricating oil Fuel oil Bitumen	48	38

What does this table tell you about some of the production problems oil refineries are faced with?

Small molecules from large molecules

The heavier fractions that are produced in surplus quantities are made of long chain hydrocarbons. Hydrocarbon molecules are made of hydrogen and carbon atoms joined together in a chain. The backbone of this chain consists of carbon atoms (see 2.9). If these long chains could be broken up into smaller sections it would provide a way of getting rid of the excess of heavier fractions and of making more of the lighter fractions.

Heating the long molecules of fuel oil and bitumen causes them to vibrate more. Continued heating will vibrate the molecules enough to break the carbon chain so that long chain molecules can be shortened. The breaking of the chain is called **cracking**. Cracking can also be induced by chemical methods, known as catalytic cracking.

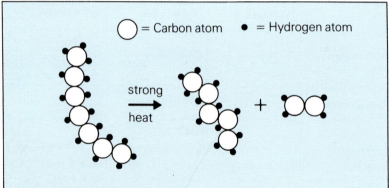

○ = Carbon atom ● = Hydrogen atom

strong heat

*Heating a hydrocarbon molecule strongly causes its carbon chain to break producing smaller molecules. This is called **cracking**.*

Cracked but useful

Cracking is a very important process because it turns the less useful fractions of crude oil like fuel oil into more widely needed fractions with smaller molecules such as petrol and paraffin. When a hydrocarbon molecule is cracked, the number of hydrogen and carbon atoms remains the same but they have been rearranged. One part of the chain contains carbon atoms all of which are surrounded by four other atoms. No more atoms can be attached and it is said to be **saturated**. Petrol and paraffin are examples of saturated molecules.

The other part of the carbon chain, produced by cracking, contains some carbon atoms surrounded by only three atoms. More atoms can still be attached to these and the molecule is said to be **unsaturated**. These unsaturated molecules are useful products from cracking. An example of an unsaturated molecule is ethene.

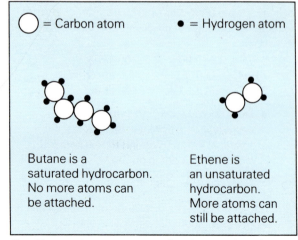

○ = Carbon atom ● = Hydrogen atom

Butane is a saturated hydrocarbon. No more atoms can be attached.

Ethene is an unsaturated hydrocarbon. More atoms can still be attached.

*Cracking produces a **saturated** and **unsaturated** hydrocarbon.*

Making giant molecules . . .

Ethene molecules can react together to form long chains containing many thousands of carbon atoms. The process of joining small molecules together to form a long chain molecule is called **polymerisation**. The chain molecule that is formed is called a **polymer** and the small molecules that are used to make it are called **monomers**. 'Poly' means 'many' so the long molecular chain that is formed of ethene units is '*poly*ethene' or *poly*thene for short. Different polymers can be made from other unsaturated molecules like styrene – *poly*styrene.

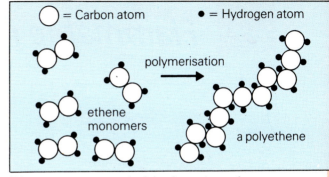

*Ethene monomers can be joined together to form polythene. This is called **polymerisation**.*

. . . to put to good use

Polythene, polystyrene, nylon are all **plastics**. We use the term plastic because of the properties of these long chain molecular materials. Plastic is really only another word for polymer. As you will notice if you look around you, today we really do live in a plastic world. . .

Different forms of plastic have different properties. Each of the properties give rise to different uses.

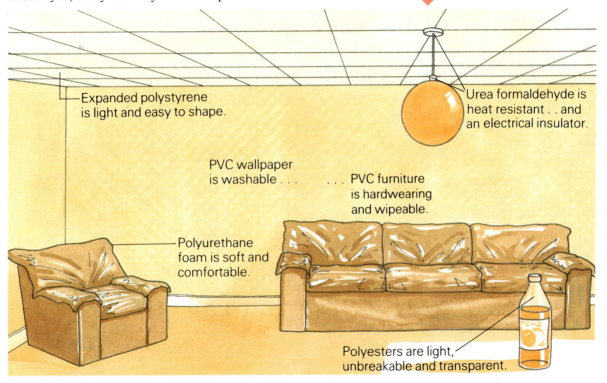

1 Look at the table at the top of the opposite page.
   a Which fractions from crude oil show a greater demand than their supply?
   b Which fraction shows the greatest shortfall between its supply and demand?
   c Why would the demand for each product change, depending on the time of year?

2 a Draw another diagram to show two different products of the cracking of the hydrocarbon.
   b Draw the shape of the polymer made from the unsaturated monomer unit which you have just drawn in part **a** above.

3 a Draw the shape of a saturated hydrocarbon containing 6 carbon atoms.
   b Draw the shape of an unsaturated hydrocarbon containing 3 carbon atoms.

4 By using catalysts, the cracking process can be made to happen much faster and at a lower temperature. Why is this so important in industry?

5 What properties of a plastic do you think make it an ideal material for a **a** watering can **b** hosepipe **c** plant pot?

6 Why do some people think the use of crude oil as a fuel is wasteful of resources?

Flammable materials

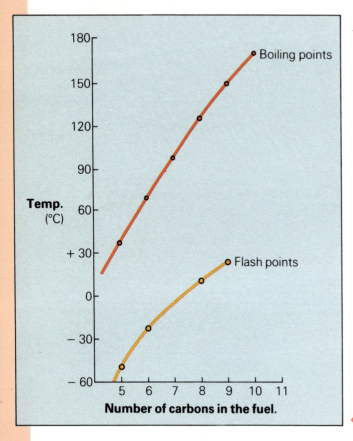

Number of carbons in the fuel.

In November 1987, 31 people died in a horrendous 'flash point' type fire at Kings Cross London Underground station. It is important for all of us to know about how different materials burn and what actually happens when they burn – fire is a very serious business.

Starting to burn

When most fuels catch fire it is the vapours from the fuel that are burning not the solid or liquid part. A petrol fire occurs in the petrol vapour, just above the surface of the liquid, not in the liquid itself. When a material is heated directly by a spark or flames the vapours will only ignite if their temperature is above a certain value. The minimum temperature above which a vapour will ignite is known as the **flash point** of the material. The harder it is to vapourise a material, the higher will be its flash point.

When vapours are compressed, for example by pistons in a diesel engine, they become hot. The more they are compressed, the hotter they become. At a certain temperature a vapour will ignite even though there is no direct source of heat. This temperature is known as the **self ignition temperature** of the material.

◀ *What does this graph show you about the flash point of a material as its boiling point increases?*

Burning up . . .

To burn a material you need oxygen, which is present in the air, and a source of heat. Materials such as petrol or natural gas which burn very easily have low flash points and are said to be highly **flammable**. Materials that don't burn are said to be **non-flammable**. Limestone, for example, is non-flammable – it breaks down into simpler substances when it is heated.

During burning, oxygen adds onto the elements of which the material is made, producing **oxides** and energy is released as heat and light. This is why there is often a flame – a mixture of heat and light – released by the burning fuel. Petrol, which is a mixture of compounds containing the elements hydrogen and carbon, burns to form water (hydrogen oxide) and carbon dioxide. The addition of oxygen to a substance is called **oxidation** and the chemical name for burning is **combustion**.

Incomplete burning

When some materials burn they often produce harmful substances because the burning has been incomplete. This incomplete burning is caused by lack of sufficient oxygen – in other words complete oxidation cannot take place. Petrol, for example, will also produce carbon monoxide (CO) and smoke or unburnt carbon (C) as well as water and carbon dioxide. Compounds which contain nitrogen as well as carbon and hydrogen such as polyurethane also produce hydrogen cyanide (HCN).

Materials need heat and oxygen before they burn.

A burning cigarette may be all that is needed to start a serious fire.

Materials which produce lots of smoke on burning contain high proportions of carbon to hydrogen. Benzene contains 6 carbons for every 6 hydrogens (C_6H_6). Methane contains 1 carbon for every 4 hydrogens (CH_4). The greater proportion of carbon to hydrogen in benzene compared with methane means that it burns with a much smokier flame than methane.

A lot of carbon in the form of soot, or smoke is produced which can make breathing very difficult.

Some furniture still contains soft padding made of polyurethane which means poisonous invisible gases such as hydrogen cyanide and carbon monoxide are produced.

Domestic fires in the home are quite common and can be very dangerous, often because of the toxic gases given off during the burning of certain materials.

Stopping the burn

To put out a fire, you need to remove the oxygen, heat or fuel. Cooling the fire by water removes the source of heat and takes the temperature of the vapours below their flash point.

Smothering a fire by using foams, powder – even a blanket, cuts off the supply of oxygen. This stops the chemical reactions occurring in the flames. However, since smothering does not cool the fuel, the temperature of the vapours could still rise above the flash point and **reignition** may occur.

Small fires may be put out using fire extinguishers. The type of extinguisher used depends on the nature and location of the fire.

Look at the table which shows 5 different types of extinguisher. Why do you think Class C fires (flammable gases) are put out by smothering-type extinguishers and not by cooling?

Type	Extinguishes mainly by	Class A fires (paper, wood, textile)	Class B fires Flammable liquids	Class C fires Flammable gases
Water	Cooling and smothering	✓	✗	✗
Foam	Smothering and cooling	✓	✓	✗
Carbon dioxide	Smothering	✗	✓	✓
Dry powder	Smothering	✓	✓	✓
Halon	Smothering	✓	✓	✓

1 Why is it dangerous to smoke near petrol but not near cooking oil?

2 Why do diesel engines not need spark plugs to ignite the fuel?

3 Look at the graph.
   a Which fuels will ignite at about room temperature (20°C)?
   b What is the boiling point and flash point of the fuel with 7 carbons?
   c What is the flash point of the fuel with 10 carbons?

4 What do you think would be formed when propane (C_3H_8) is burnt **a** completely **b** incompletely?

5 Which fuel will burn with the smokier flame, propane (C_3H_8) or toluene (C_7H_8)?

6 a What do you think are the most likely causes of death in domestic fires?
   b What do you think are the most likely cause of these fires?

7 Look at the table.
   a Which extinguishers can only be used for class A fires?
   b Which extinguisher do you think give the least risk of the fuel reigniting?
   c Which types of extinguisher would you *not* use if your chip pan full of very hot oil caught fire? What could you do if you did not have a suitable extinguisher to hand?

Rotten materials

You can eat apples but so can tiny organisms such as bacteria and fungi, causing the fruit to rot.

Wet rot is very easy to control when the source of dampness has been removed . . . .

Dry rot is harder to control because it can spread across brickwork and iron or lie 'dormant' for years.

Rotting away

You eat apples when they are fresh and ripe . . . but apples are also a source of food for other tiny organisms (micro-organisms). These organisms are so small you can't see them and so light they are easily carried by the wind from place to place – they are in fact all around us. You can, however, see a fungus when it multiplies rapidly from its spores on food. Fungi also feed on other materials such as wood and paper. When a material, such as an apple is being "eaten" by fungi and bacteria the material is said to be **rotting**.

Decayed wood eventually becomes part of the soil.

Wanted rot

Fungi and other micro-organisms, such as bacteria, are nature's scavengers. In damp conditions, they rot dead materials, for example wood leaves and manure. When these materials rot they are broken down into simpler substances which get added to the soil as **nutrients**. This is part of nature's recycling process. These materials, which can be broken down naturally, are said to be **biodegradable**. Many synthetic materials such as most plastics cannot be broken down by fungi or bacteria. They are said to be **non-biodegradable**.

Unwanted rot

Fungi will also rot the wood that is used in buildings. As a result the wood loses some of its important properties such as strength and toughness. When fungi land on a piece of wood they grow and throw out hollow tubes called hyphae. These hyphae are able to penetrate the wood. As they do they produce chemicals that are able to break down the materials in the wood into simpler substances. The fungi are able to digest these simple substances, allowing them to grow and spread further through the wood, and so destroy its strength and toughness further.

The two most common types of rot found in wood in buildings are wet rot and dry rot. How do you think they got their names?

Looking at wood

All plants need to stand upright to some extent so that their leaves can get plenty of light for photosynthesis (see 4.6). Plants contain cellulose in the walls of their cells to make the stem strong and flexible. In certain plants a substance called **lignin** is added to the cellulose in the cell walls. These lignified cells are what we call wood.

Looking closely at the elements of the cells of wood we can see how it is such a tough and strong material.

The hollow cells of wood are joined together to make long tubes like drainpipes. This makes the stems of plants, like trees and shrubs, strong and rigid.

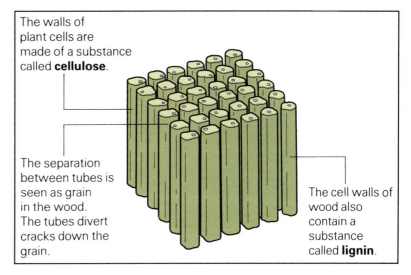

The walls of plant cells are made of a substance called **cellulose**.

The separation between tubes is seen as grain in the wood. The tubes divert cracks down the grain.

The cell walls of wood also contain a substance called **lignin**.

The cellulose forms white stringy fibres which are flexible and strong. When partly broken down they become crumbly.

Lignin is a dark brown resin. It cements the cellulose fibres together.

Lignin makes wood tough and strong. The more cellulose fibres, the harder the wood is to crack.

Under attack

When a fungus attacks wood the hyphae of the fungus penetrate through the wood, boring their way from fibre to fibre so that the cell walls are partially or completely eaten away.

Fungus	Effect on wood
A	leaves the wood white and stringy
B	causes the wood to crack very easily
C	leaves the wood light brown but it cracks across the grain, not down it

1   Why is it very difficult to kill all fungi?

2   Why is timber left to dry out or 'season' before being used for building material.

3   Why is wood rot a problem and why is dry rot more serious than wet rot?

4   Why is plastic rubbish a problem and how might it be solved?

5   Look at the table above.
   a What is being eaten by fungus A? What properties do you expect the wood to have?
   b What colour would the wood be after attack by fungus B? Why does it crack very easily? What is being eaten by fungus B?
   c Why are the cracks in the wood attacked by fungus C able to spread across the grain and not get diverted down the grain? What is being eaten by fungus C?

2.13

Metals

Metals are useful materials . . .

Metals have characteristic properties that make them useful.

 Metals like aluminium are **ductile**. They can be drawn out into wires or cables.

Metals such as aluminium or copper are good conductors of heat.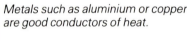

Steel, a mixture of iron and carbon, is **malleable**. It can be easily shaped.

Silver globules of mercury can be obtained from red mercuric oxide by heating.

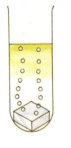   

Zinc   Silver   Magnesium

This diagram shows what happens when three different metals are placed in acid. What does it show you about the reactivity of magnesium compared to the other two metals?

. . . . locked into ores

Some metals, such as gold, are found as "free" metals – that is pure metals – not chemically combined to other elements. Metals such as gold do not combine easily with other elements. However, most metals are found in the Earth chemically combined with other elements in the form of a compound called a **metal ore.** The metal then has to be **extracted** from the ore. Oxygen and sulphur are two elements that are often present in ores, tightly combined with the metal. For example, iron and oxygen combine together to form the ore, haematite, which has the chemical name iron oxide. This compound has completely different properties to the original elements iron and oxygen.

There are three ways of separating metals from the other elements present in ores – using heat, chemical or electrical energy.

The reactivity of metals

Some metals are more **reactive** than others. This means they can be chemically changed very easily. In order to separate a metal from its ore chemically, use is made of differences in reactivity. Some metals react with acids, releasing bubbles of hydrogen gas. The more reactive the metal, the more hydrogen is produced.

The league table of reactivity

By looking at other reactions involving metals, the metals can be placed in a league table of reactivity called the **reactivity series**. The higher a metal's position in the league table, the more reactive it is. Look at the table. It can help you to predict the reactivity of different metals with acids.

Using chemical energy-competition reactions

If two metals compete for the same element, the more reactive element *always* "wins" the competition. Thus the reactivity series can be used to dislodge a wanted metal from its ore, by using a more reactive metal. For example if aluminium and iron oxide (haematite) are heated together, molten iron and aluminium oxide are produced. The aluminium is higher in the reactivity series and so is more reactive than the iron. The aluminium will compete with the iron for the oxygen and will "grab" the oxygen from the iron to give pure iron and aluminium oxide. This is called a **competition reaction**.

Using electrical energy

Sometimes it is not possible to supply enough chemical and heat energy to obtain metals from their ores. This is particularly true when trying to obtain metals at the top of the reactivity series from their ores. Aluminium could not be obtained from its ore by a competition reaction with zinc since zinc is less reactive than aluminium. In such cases electrical energy can provide all the energy that is needed. The electricity is passed through the hot molten ore. The energy provided by the electricity is sufficient to separate the metal from its ore.

Non metal elements can also be used in competition reactions. Coke is a form of carbon and when heated to high temperatures in a blast furnace the carbon (in the hot coke) will remove oxygen from the iron oxide producing molten iron.

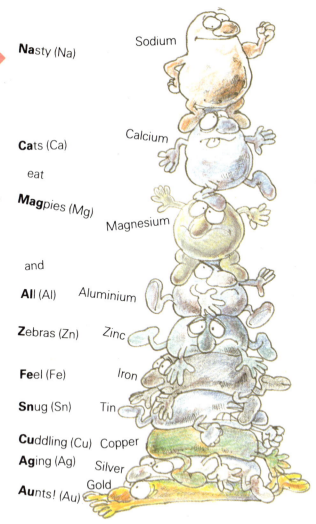

Nasty (Na) — Sodium
Cats (Ca) — Calcium
eat
Magpies (Mg) — Magnesium
and
All (Al) — Aluminium
Zebras (Zn) — Zinc
Feel (Fe) — Iron
Snug (Sn) — Tin
Cuddling (Cu) — Copper
Aging (Ag) — Silver
Aunts! (Au) — Gold

Maybe this will help you remember the reactivity series!

1   State two properties of metals and one example of how each property is used.

2   Why is gold found as a "free" metal and not combined with oxygen?

3   Look at the diagram on the opposite page.
   a Place the three metals in order of reactivity, starting with the most reactive first.
   b Predict which metals would react with acids more vigorously than magnesium.
   c Suggest a metal that you think will not react with acids.
   d If you had to test your answer to **b** and **c** what conditions are needed to make sure the test would be fair?

4   a Where would you place carbon in the reactivity series?
   b Why can't carbon be used to obtain aluminium from aluminium oxide?
   c Name a metal that could be used to obtain aluminium from aluminium oxide in a competition reaction.
   d Name an alternative method of obtaining aluminium from aluminium oxide.

2.14

Corrosion of metals

Corroding away

Metals are very important materials but under certain conditions they can be changed to compounds with less useful properties. When this occurs the metals are said to **corrode** and have to be replaced or discarded. Rusting is the particular name given to the corrosion of iron.

Some corroded metals are also dull. They lose their attractive appearance.

When a metal such as copper corrodes it is no longer as good a conductor of electricity.

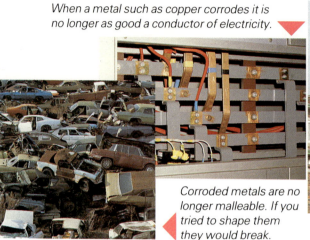

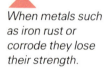

When metals such as iron rust or corrode they lose their strength.

Corroded metals are no longer malleable. If you tried to shape them they would break.

Conditions for rusting

A group of students decided to investigate what conditions are needed for rusting. They put some iron nails into test tubes containing different substances and then left them for a few days. These diagrams show the results the students obtained. What did they decide was always needed for rusting to occur?

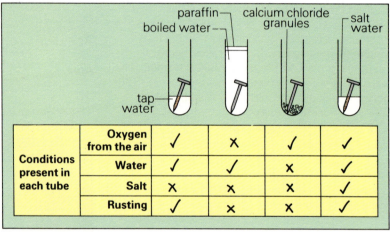

Conditions present in each tube		tap water / boiled water paraffin	calcium chloride granules	salt water
	Oxygen from the air	✓	✗	✓	✓
	Water	✓	✓	✗	✓
	Salt	✗	✗	✗	✓
	Rusting	✓	✗	✗	✓

These diagrams show the results the students obtained. What do you think they decided was always needed for rusting to occur?

Stopping the rust

One way to prevent iron from rusting is to seal its surface. This protects the iron from chemical attack by the oxygen and water which cause rusting. However, once the seal is broken the unprotected iron will rust. This causes the surface to blister, exposing fresh iron so the rusting continues.

Oil lubricates the chain but also protects it.

Paint protects the frame.

Chrome protects the chain wheel and parts of the wheels and handlebar.

Rusting can be prevented in a number of different ways.

What a sacrifice!

A more effective way of preventing iron rusting is to use **sacrificial protection**. A metal which is more reactive than iron, such as zinc, is painted onto the surface of the iron. (Look at the reactivity series on p.59). Because zinc is higher in the reactivity series it reacts first and corrodes instead of the iron. It "sacrifices" itself for the iron. If the surface is scratched or only partly covered, the zinc still provides protection from rusting because the water and oxygen will react with the zinc first, even if there is iron around.

The same group of students carried out another series of experiments to test the process of sacrificial protection. These diagrams show the results they obtained after leaving the samples in plain water for a few days.

Zinc is bolted onto a ships hull. It rusts instead of iron because it is more reactive.

What do these results tell you about the reactivity of tin compared to iron?

Self protection

Some metals, like aluminium, protect themselves by forming a protective oxide layer which blocks further corrosion.

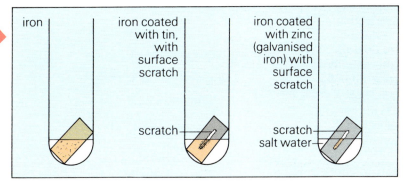

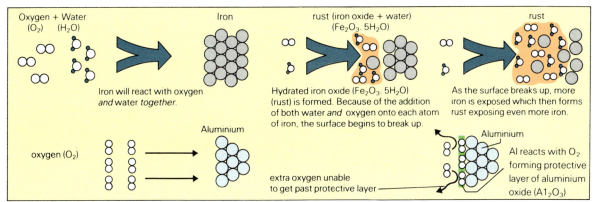

---

1 Why does rusting cost the country millions of pounds every year?

2 In the first of the students' investigations:
   a what do you think is the purpose of
      i the calcium chloride granules
      ii the paraffin
   b why was the water boiled?
   c what effect did salt water appear to have on rusting?

3 If chromium only provides protection from rust until it is scratched, what does this tell you about its reactivity compared to iron?

4 Name another metal that could have been bolted onto the ship's hull instead of zinc. Give a reason for your answer.

5 In the second of the students' investigations:
   a what did the group need to do to make sure the test is fair?
   b what do the results tell you about the reactivity of zinc compared to iron?
   c what would have happened if the iron had been coated in copper instead of zinc?

6 Why don't aluminium window frames corrode?

Index *(refers to spread numbers)*

For additional information, see the following modules:
6   Making the most of Machines
8   Structure and Bonding
9   Chemical Patterns

Photo acknowledgements

These refer to the spread number and, where appropriate, the photo order:

Barnaby's Picture Library *2.9/1, 2.10, 2.14/3, 2.15/1, 2.15/5, 2.15/6;* Buildings Research Establishment *2.13/4;* J. Allan Cash *2.5, 2.14/5;* CEGB *2.14/2;* GeoScience Features *2.13/3;* Sally and Richard Greenhill *2.2/1, 2.2/2, 2.9/2, 2.14/3;* Trevor Hill *2.2/3, 2.6, 2.8/1, 2.8/3, 2.9/3, 2.15/3, 2.15/4;* Eric and David Hosking *2.13/2;* Colin Johnson *2.14/4;* Frank Lane Agency (RogerWilmhurst) *2.13/1;* Science Photo Library *2.8/2, 2.15/2.*
Picture Researcher: Jennifer Johnson